HOME END

SCENES FROM THE FINAL DAYS OF A TRADITIONAL ENGLISH FOOTBALL GROUND

TONY COLE

© Tony Cole, 2018

Published by Yorktonebooks

For further information contact yorktonebooks@gmail.com or via Twitter @Yorktone

All rights reserved. No part of this book may be reproduced, adapted, stored in a retrieval system or transmitted by any means, electronic, mechanical, photocopying, or otherwise without the prior written permission of the author.

The rights of Tony Cole to be identified as the author of this work
have been asserted in accordance with the Copyright, Designs and Patents Act 1988.

A CIP catalogue record for this book is available from the British Library.

ISBN 978-1-5272-3414-7

Book layout by Clare Brayshaw

Prepared and printed by:

York Publishing Services Ltd
64 Hallfield Road
Layerthorpe
York YO31 7ZQ

Tel: 01904 431213

www.yps-publishing.co.uk

This book is dedicated to the supporters of York City FC past, present and future, but particularly to Greg, Richard and Robbo in whose company I have spent many, many hours and yet still too few. Cheers lads. Also to Lou, to my boy Ed and my girls Jules and Mo – see, I made a book!

Foreword

I first came across Tony Cole's photographs three or four years ago when we started following each other on Twitter. He had been to see a production of my play Port, and his enthusiasm for it, even in that most heated of forums, was moving. He sounded like a kindred spirit. His work assured me that he was more than that. We look at the world, it seems to me, from the same perspective.

The photos he shares on that forum are tough and tender at the same time. Carved out of the edges of London and York, they are portraits of the drunk and despairing, the heartbroken and hilarious. They were made out of the same tension between admiration and clarity that I aspire to in my plays.

I have been inspired by photography for two decades. The photographers I like carry an innate drama in their work. They capture a moment of humanity in action. They pause it briefly. They slice through it. This is something that I have tried to do in my plays, and the first play that I tried to do this with was Port. In the making of that play I returned again and again to the photographs of the great American realist William Egglestone. In his framing of the ordinary I found something I wanted to reach for. Maybe that was what Tony recognised in my play.

Maybe he recognised the representation of York. I studied for three years at York University. As a campus university, it grazes its host city in the same way the touristic hub of the Minster and Shambles do. I realised during my time there that both the campus and the medieval theme park were artificial places adjoined to the town. I remembered the town I lived in on seeing Cole's photography.

There is a line in Port when one character compares York to the play's setting, my home town of Stockport. Often in performance, this line got a laugh. It was a laugh I never enjoyed. It was a laugh assuming that the comparison between Stockport and York was in some way silly. I never found it so; these were two towns that strongly reminded me of one another. York, to my mind, was not a place of tea shops and thousand-year-old churches. Yes, they were there, and they defined a trace through it, but York, like Stockport, was a place of cheap supermarkets and cheap booze; tense pubs and violent nightclubs; barely dressed drunks in winter, charming exhausted cabbies and canny dealers.

It is a stratum of England that has been perceived as divisive over the past decade or so. The subjects of this book are mainly men, mainly white men at that. They are hewn from the North. They are brought together of different ages. They seem to be always dressed for the cold. This is a book that looks at the working-class white men of the north of England and, through their photographer's clear eye, finds in them the possibility of some kind of grace.

A certain spirit characterises lower-league football clubs too. Not for York City or Stockport County the glory and dollar of the Premier League. These are vulnerable clubs of weathered terraces and flat beer. These are clubs built on loyalty and irony, dry wit, black humour, a long, latent simmer of something about to kick off and the possible euphoria of the impossible goal. These are the subjects of Tony's work.

Looking at the photographs collected here I am struck by something that unites all football clubs. It unites even the moneyed stadia of the monolithic forces of the Champions League. At football games strangers are bought together, for a while, to look in the same direction at the same time and share an experience. It is in this experience, this commitment to a shared story, that the grace Tony realises is located, I think.

And it is, like the condemned stadium, vulnerable. I may be wrong but, from memory, I can think of no images of the people in these photographs looking at their phones. In spite of the stinking toilets and the holes in the roof these are people engaged in the same story at the same time. If this engagement is under threat from an era of new technology and the promise of a new community stadium, or preyed on by the divisive seduction and spite of the nationalist right, it is a spirit that defines the photography of Tony Cole and that in his work I think will find an invulnerability.

Simon Stephens

London, April 2018

Introduction

For roughly 35 years I have supported York City FC with varying degrees of dedication or indifference that seem to have almost always led me to miss the achievements and witness seemingly endless periods of mediocrity, or worse. I've watched an ever-changing cast of players who, with some honourable exceptions, have left an indelible blank on my memory. Leagues have come and gone. Relegations have outnumbered promotions. Managerial eras have risen and fallen. But there has been one constant: Bootham Crescent, home of York City FC since 1932.

In 2019 Bootham Crescent will close. The site it occupies will be sold and redeveloped as a housing estate. York City FC will move to a purpose-built all-seater stadium on the Monks Cross retail park at the edge of the city. For reasons still not entirely clear to me – though certainly influenced by the fact that nobody else seemed interested in doing so – I decided to try to record a bit of the old place and the people who call it home before the terraces fall silent for the final time.

I hope these scenes from the final days of a traditional English football ground will show that, at a time when football is being relentlessly cleansed of its working-class origins, there are a few remaining places (now one fewer) where you can sometimes glimpse what generations past cared enough to create, and we, by mortgaging them against illusory and ultimately meaningless success, have allowed to be destroyed. In these pictures you will find nothing spectacular. The very ordinariness of the people and the backdrop they appear against should be recorded precisely because it so ordinary.

In the poem 'I remember, I remember' Philip Larkin states that 'nothing, like something, happens anywhere', and that feeling of absolute English ordinariness permeates Bootham Crescent. For me, that has a beauty and a value that can never be replicated or replaced.

Football is a beautiful sport, not a business. It has lost its way.

Tony Cole

September 2018

HOME END

SCENES FROM THE FINAL DAYS OF A TRADITIONAL ENGLISH FOOTBALL GROUND

ROAD AHEAD CLOSED

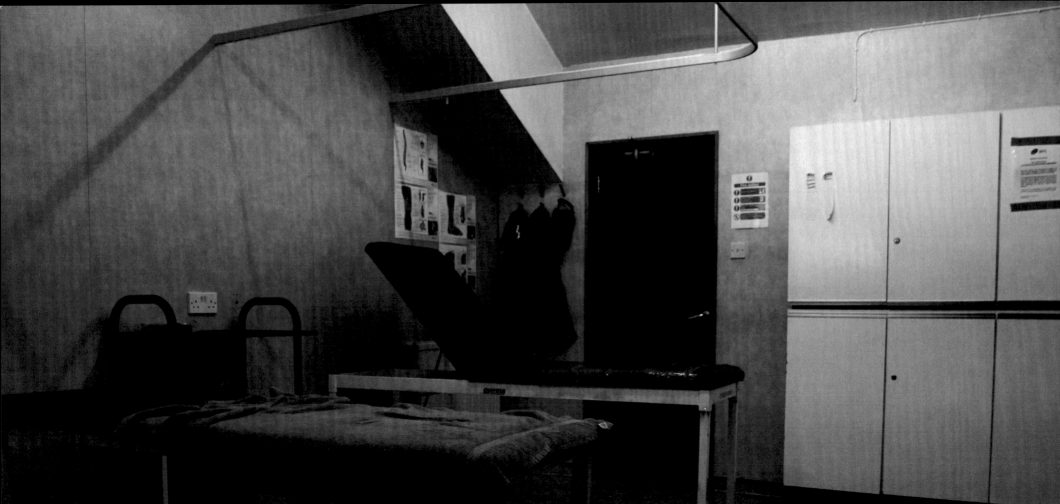

IF THE SHOWERS ARE
COLD, RUN THE BATH
UNTIL THE WATER GETS
HOT.

THEN SWITCH OFF THE
BATH AND TURN ON THE
SHOWERS AND THE
WATER IN THE
SHOWERS WILL BE HOT!

**PLEASE DO
NOT CLEAN
BOOTS IN
THE SINK**

HOME

GATE
A

ROAD
AHEAD
CLOSED

Thanks and acknowledgements

I think it was 2017 when I first tweeted a couple of pictures of Bootham Crescent. Rather flatteringly it wasn't long before people started to follow my @yorktone account and comment positively on the images in which they often recognised themselves or their mates and family. Social media is a wonder (and terror) of our age. For those of us who grew up pre internet it's hard not to marvel at how simply we – from plebs to plutocrats – can now communicate ideas, spew opinions and generously share our artistic impulses for free with virtually no thought or effort whatsoever. So it was in that spirit of lazy complacency that I decided to make a book of images relating to that most hapless and unfortunate football club, York City FC.

Along the way I had some good ideas that were impractical and some bad ideas that led me into numerous dog-shit alleys of frustration. Perhaps my best, but least practical idea, was to ask for contributions to the book from fellow City fans. These were to be coupled with my images to create a sort of emotional coda that would demonstrate the absurdly one-sided love affair we have with a football club that all too often rewards our devotion with only cold indifference, disappointment and mad rules regarding the removal of bottle tops.

Lots of people were kind enough to submit contributions ranging from tweet length micro rants to lengthy essays on love and despair in a relegation season. Alas I was insufficiently skilled to make the idea work in a format that was coherent and affordable. All the contributors are listed below. I want to ensure that they are both acknowledged for their efforts but also sincerely thanked from the bottom of my heart for their belief and support and for the many interesting and funny online and face-to face conversations the mad idea generated. They are…

Harriet Whittam, Simon Pickering, Tom Poole, John Dobson, Adam Livingston, Dean Wade, Tom Haugh, Tim Milburn, Rob Howarth, Alex Fox, George Gregory, Will Harris, George Mallet, Shaun Urquhart, Rob Lee, Andrew Leathley, Sam 'Happy Wanderer' Radcliffe, Paul Jobson, Phil Bedford, Mike Carroll, Richard Atkinson, Alan Raimes, Marie Barker, Clare Feasby, Roy Clarkson. Russ Hoban, Terry Espiner, Alex Bedingham, Steve Castle, Paul Clelland, Jack Crabtree, Stephen Jones, Charlotte Halstead, Neil Hiffins, Neil Ferguson, Tom Putnam, David Towler, James Richardson, Ciaron Forrest, David Holder, Jon Rawnsley and Mike Parker.

Special thanks to the following for practical assistance and support – Duncan Beale at York Publishing, Phil Howden for allowing me access to the stadium one memorable March morning, Joe Haining who, at a moment's notice, edited and honestly appraised my efforts to write an introduction. Michael Elgie for putting together some initial visuals for the book. Michael Miles of Y-Front fanzine for his constant support and encouragement and almost last, but definitely not least, my brother Fred for making the whole reckless endeavour possible with hard cash and kind words.

And so, finally, I want to acknowledge and thank Simon Stephens for his brilliant and insightful foreword – an honour I still feel is undeserved.

I first saw Simon's play *Port* in 2013. Simon had collaborated with the ace photographer Kevin Cummins to run a street photography competition alongside the play's run at the National Theatre in London. A theatregoing colleague at work had shown me a flyer and I thought I'd chance my arm by submitting a couple of images. Astonishingly a shortlisted place among the finalists ensured a pair of free tickets to see the play.

Along I went with a mate from work and was instantly impressed and moved by the clarity with which Stephens wrote about, and dramatized, the lives of people who looked and sounded like I did, and who played out their extraordinary ordinariness against backdrops of bus shelters and beer gardens in a way that I not only completely related to, but had tried hard (and failed) to capture in my photography. The fact that in the middle of the play York City get a mention sealed the deal. I'm indebted forever.

At the end of Simon's play Sea Wall, the play's sole on-stage character Alex, a photographer, delivers the following lines…

> *"There's a lie at the heart of photography that I've always cherished. When you take a photograph what you do is you freeze something that's actually alive. To do this properly you need, more than anything, to believe in life."*

For me there were never truer words.

Thank you all.

TC